A little book of God's blessings to you both

Gracie Shooting Straight from the Heart

GRACIE SHOOTING STRAIGHT FROM THE HEART

ISBN 0-85009-127-6 (Australia 1-86258-025-1)

Printed in Italy.
Worldwide co-edition organised and produced by Angus Hudson Ltd, London.

WORD PUBLISHING
Word (UK) Ltd
England

Word Books Australia, Sunday School Centre Wholesale
South Africa, Alby Commercial Enterprises Pte Ltd
Singapore, Concorde Distributors Ltd New Zealand,
Cross (HK) Company Hong Kong, Eunsung Corp Korea,
Praise Inc Philippines.

Gracie

HAS A MESSAGE OF LOVE
JUST FOR YOU FROM
THE HEART OF YOUR
FATHER
IN
HEAVEN

ALWAYS REMEMBER...

PSALM 139:13

GOD CREATED YOU
... AND YOU ARE
WONDERFULLY MADE

... AND HE ONLY MADE
ONE OF YOU

I THESS. 4:9

GOD HIMSELF WILL
TEACH YOU HOW TO LOVE

IMAGINE... LESSONS FROM
THE MASTER

ROMANS 8:39

NOTHING WILL BE ABLE
TO SEPARATE YOU FROM
HIS LOVE IN JESUS

A PERFECT LOVE
... YOURS FOREVER

ROMANS 5:5

GOD HAS POURED
HIS LOVE INTO OUR HEARTS
BY HIS SPIRIT

...HIS LOVE
HIS WONDERFUL LOVE

I JOHN 4:12

WHEN WE LOVE ANOTHER
... GOD'S LOVE IS MADE
PERFECT IN US

SO WHEN YOU LOVE
SOMEONE ... TELL THEM!

I COR. 13:14

LOVE IS PATIENT
AND KIND

ALWAYS MAKE TIME
TO SHOW IT

EPHESIANS 5:2

. . . AND WALK IN LOVE
JUST AS CHRIST
LOVED YOU

IT'S A PERFECT PATH
. . . IT DOESN'T GO ASTRAY

COL. 2:2

THAT THEIR HEARTS
MIGHT BE HAPPY, BEING
KNIT TOGETHER
IN LOVE

YOU ARE PART OF HIS PATTERN!

1 COR. 13:8

LOVE NEVER FAILS

A RECIPE THAT CAN'T GO WRONG

I JOHN 3:18

DON'T JUST LOVE IN WORDS ... SHOW IT IN KIND DEEDS

SOMEBODY NEEDS YOU!

I COR. 14:1

PURSUE LOVE
... MAKE IT
YOUR AIM

REMEMBER
... PRACTICE MAKES
PERFEC

PSALM 36:7

HOW PRECIOUS
IS YOUR STEADFAST LOVE
O GOD

NEVER FORGET IT
... YOU ARE LOVED!

... JUST REMEMBER
TO PASS
IT ON!